A LOOK AT LIFE FROM
a Deer Stand

STEVE CHAPMAN
paintings by the
HAUTMAN BROTHERS

HARVEST HOUSE PUBLISHERS

EUGENE, OREGON

A Look at Life from a Deer Stand—Gift Edition

Text copyright © 2005 by Steve Chapman
Published by Harvest House Publishers
Eugene, Oregon 97402

Library of Congress Cataloging-in-Publication Data

Chapman, Steve.
    A look at life from a deer stand / text by Steve Chapman ; artwork by
the Hautman brothers.—Gift ed.
        p. cm.
    ISBN 978-0-7369-1488-8
    1. White-tailed deer hunting—Tennessee—Anecdotes. 2. Conduct of life—Anecdotes. I. Title.
    SK301.C514 2005
    799.2'7652—dc22

                                    2004015701

Artwork designs are reproduced under license from © 2005 by The Hautman Brothers, courtesy of MHS
Licensing, and may not be reproduced without permission.

Design and production by Koechel Peterson & Associates, Minneapolis, Minnesota

Harvest House Publishers has made every effort to trace the ownership of all poems and quotes. In the
event of a question arising from the use of a poem or quote, we regret any error made and will be pleased
to make the necessary correction in future editions of this book.

Portions of this text are excerpted from *A Look at Life from a Deer Stand* by Steve Chapman (Harvest
House Publishers, 1998).

Unless otherwise indicated, Scripture verses are taken from the New American Standard Bible®, © 1960,
1962, 1963, 1968, 1971, 1972, 1973, 1975, 1977 by The Lockman Foundation. Used by permission.
(www.Lockman.org)

Printed in China

10 11 12 / NG / 15 14 13 12 11 10

Today, look around you, set your distance markers, appreciate the hunting ground you're allowed, work on your shooting ability, and trust the Creator of this vast universe to increase your range as time goes on.

Happy hunting!

FIRST WINDS OF AUTUMN

When the green of the cornstalk
Begins to turn brown
When the time for the goldenrod bloom comes around
That's when I look at the hills, for I know
Soon I'll walk there again
With my arrow and bow.

When the fruit of the white oak
Is ready to fall
And when the hummingbird feels
That old Mexico call
And when the tears touch the cheeks
Of my sweetheart she knows
Soon it's farewell to her man
With the arrow and bow.

The heart of the hunter who can explain
How the first winds of autumn
Seem to whisper my name
And sends me to dreamin'
'Bout the morning I'll go
Back up to the hills
With my arrow and bow.

Steve Chapman

ADRENALINE PIE

BASK FOR A FEW MOMENTS IN THE WONDERFUL WORLD OF THE GREAT OUTDOORS. IT IS A VERY SPECIAL GIFT FROM GOD, PRESERVED BY OUR FOREFATHERS TO BE SHARED AND ENJOYED BY EACH OF US AND ALL GENERATIONS TO COME.

Jack Terry

The dry, fallen leaves lightly crunched on the ground behind the tree I was perched in, and my heart started to race. I knew that sound. It was not a squirrel or a busy chipmunk stirring back there. The sound was unique. I had heard it before. I didn't move a muscle, even though everything within me wanted to shift my body to take a look. I fought my instincts and sat motionless, gripping my compound bow in my nervous hand and rehearsing the steps to pull to a full draw.

It seemed like an hour before I heard the next step, though I knew that less than a minute had passed. These situations always make life seem longer. I turned my eyes in their sockets as far right as I could and hoped for movement. Sure enough, I saw a form move and then stop. As slowly as a shadow on a sundial, I rotated my head and looked down. Eighteen feet below my treestand stood the creature I had been waiting for. It was an eight-point white-tailed buck deer. What a rush!

My wait to spot such a magnificent creature had not begun that morning 30 minutes before daylight. Instead, my vigil started the day hunting season had ended the year before. I was, to put it

honestly, addicted to the rush of excitement I felt in that moment. Getting close enough to hear the cautious footsteps of one of the smartest animals on the earth is absolutely intoxicating. Add to that ingredient an attempt to inflict the animal with a fatal wound using a primitive weapon like a bow and arrow, and you have the makings of adrenaline pie. I was loving it!

> There is a passion
>
> for hunting something
>
> deeply implanted in the
>
> human breast.
>
> *Charles Dickens*

LIFE IS A LOT *like a day in the woods.*

It has a beginning and an end. We take the alpha with the omega. The firstborn will leave home. Someday there'll be a final step. There'll be a last kiss, a last word, a graduation, a good-bye, a sunset, and—brace yourself—there'll even be a last hunt. When will it be? Who knows?

FATHOMLESS FUN

Every time I walk into the woods, I learn something new. It really is

one of the joys of the activity. While some people would be absolutely

bored out of their minds sitting for hours hoping to get close to a deer,

I find that it is full of fathomless fun. Unlike the pilot that said, "Flying

is hours and hours of boredom interrupted by moments of stark fear,"

deer hunting is hours and hours of sweet anticipation graced with

moments of incredible excitement.

Any relation to the land, the habit of tilling it,
or mining it, or even hunting on it, generates
the feeling of patriotism.

Ralph Waldo Emerson

James Hautman ©

HUNTING GOD IS A GREAT ADVENTURE.

Marie de Floris

LESSONS FROM A HUNTING MENTOR

About 20 minutes before daylight, we stopped by a large oak. My hunting mentor, Kenneth Bledsoe, took his foot and with his big boot he scraped away the dry leaves on the forest floor to reveal an area of dark, soft ground about three feet wide and three feet long. He said softly, "You'll need a quiet place to sit. You don't want to be making a lot of noise while you hunt. You're in the critters' territory. They know sounds. Unfamiliar noises are a sign of danger to them. Now, have a seat here and try to move only when it's time to take a shot." Then, as if I were being left on a deserted island, he walked up the hill behind me and out of sight. Just before he left, he whispered, "I'll be around the hill. Stay here till I come back and get you."

It was the next 30 to 40 minutes that forever sealed the joy of hunting in my heart. There I sat, outside, under a tree as the world came to life. Creatures began to respond to the rays of the sun

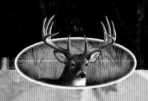

that crept over the top of the ridge. With each passing minute, an excitement started to build inside me. I heard all kinds of sounds I had never heard before. Crows were cawing in the distance, speaking an unknown language. Leaves were mysteriously rustling on the ground somewhere nearby, a hoot owl made its call, and an amazing variety of birds began to sing their tunes. Like a city going to work, the animals that didn't work the night shift (like raccoons and possums) began their foraging for food. It was absolutely amazing to me that such a kingdom existed and that I was sitting in the middle of it.

After the hunt was over, on the way back to the house, Kenneth began to teach me the art of stalking through the woods. He showed me how to pick a place void of fallen twigs, put the toe down first, and then set the rest of the foot down gently. He instructed me to not forget to stop often and keep the eyes moving like radar across the woods. The techniques I gleaned from his seasoned wisdom that morning have yielded some impressive mounts that hang on my walls today.

In hunting through a new country a man should, if possible, choose some prominent landmarks, and then should learn how they look from different sides—for they will with difficulty be recognized as the same objects, if seen from different points of view. If he gets out of sight of these, he should choose another to work back to, as a kind of half-way point; and so on. He should keep looking back; it is wonderful how different a country looks when following back on one's trail.

Theodore Roosevelt

A PARENTING GUIDE

I really didn't mind that by the time I reached the stand of trees and set up my portable treestand, I was in a drenching sweat. I was happy just to be on that wooded hillside in Cheatham County, Tennessee. At that time in my life, I was a novice bow hunter. I immediately was consumed by it. I knew very little but wanted to learn it all. So I spent days—even weeks—getting ready for the season. I loved every part of it—even the sweat. I had a pawnshop Bear Whitetail compound bow and some arrows I had found at a garage sale.

At the time our children were very young. In fact, one was "in the oven." Heidi was due in a few months, and Nathan was not yet three years old. I'm not sure how many children it takes to fill the proverbial quiver, but ours was full with two. I am very grateful for them and love them both with all of my heart. Early on in my fatherhood, I had a strong desire to be the best dad I could be, but I couldn't see a mistake I was making. I was allowing my new interest in archery to threaten the time and attention that belonged to my children.

Sitting in that treestand, I waited from sunup till about 9:30 AM. There was no movement, no noise—just dead silence. I was having a problem staying awake. I know I dozed off several times. In fact, during one snooze that probably lasted 30 seconds but seemed like an hour, I found myself dreaming. When I opened my eyes, all I could see was the ground about 20 feet below. I thought I was falling, and it startled me to the point I gasped loudly. I immediately realized where I was and began to laugh.

I needed a way to stay awake, so I took the opportunity to check out my equipment. The compound bow cams, cables, grip, sights, silencers, and the broadhead tip all seemed to be in order. I then eyed the arrow for straightness, and that's when a phrase passed through my head. It sounded so good in my thoughts that I said it out loud: "the arrow and the bow." Somehow it sounded melodic to me, more so than "bow and arrow." As a songwriter, I'm always considering how words are metered together, and this phrase grabbed my attention. I thought to myself, "I'd like to use those words in a song someday."

> There's no delight
>
> by day or night
>
> Than hunting
>
> in the morn.
>
> *William Roscoe Thayer*

My attention kept going back to that phrase "the arrow and the bow." I began to ponder the meaning, and a sobering analogy came to mind. *The bow is like the parent and the arrow is like the child.* A flood of thoughts followed. First, there will come a day when I'll have to let my children go. Just like I draw back the arrow and release it at the right moment, so it should be that I release my children at the right time. I don't look forward to that day, but if things go normally, they'll eventually leave. The "drawing back" starts early in their lives. Second, at what target am I aiming my arrows? If I want their lives to be placed in the center of God's will, then that's where I must aim. What am I doing to help make it so?

EASY VENISON STEW

The Recipe

I saw the deer

And took its life

Then gave it to

My skillful wife

She added leeks

And tall morels

A secret spice

I dare not tell

And deep red fruit

Of tomato vines

Legumes and fire

And evening time

Bread of wheat

And coffee hot...

She made me glad

I took the shot!

Steve Chapman

2-3	lbs. venison cubes
1	tablespoon salt
2	tablespoons Worcestershire sauce
2	teaspoons Liquid Smoke
4	medium potatoes, cubed
6	medium carrots, sliced
4	stalks celery, chopped
2	teaspoons minced garlic
4	tablespoons olive oil
1	envelope Lipton Onion Soup Mix
6	cups water
3	tablespoons cornstarch

Rinse venison and pat dry. Heat oil in Dutch oven to medium high. Rub meat with salt, half of Liquid Smoke, and Worcestershire sauce. Brown meat until all the liquid is absorbed. Add water, soup mix, and garlic and let simmer for 1 1/2 hours. Add potatoes, carrots, and celery; simmer until tender. Just prior to serving, add remaining Liquid Smoke. Spoon out about 1/2 cup of the broth and put into jar. Add cornstarch and shake until smooth. Stir mixture back into broth to thicken.

LIVING OUT TALL TALES

I finally settled into my stand about daylight and began the wait. Around 8:00 AM, a large doe came within range. I slowly pulled back, took careful aim, and let the arrow fly. I meant to hit the doe, but I honestly didn't see the tree I killed. That baby weighed in at around 2000 pounds field dressed. I was devastated and embarrassed, even though no one was around to witness the errant shot. I thought my hunt was over, but at 8:30 two more deer came by. I took aim and pushed the release button, sending the arrow on its way. I missed the deer but I killed the earth. Yes, sir! I hit it dead center! It weighed in at 6000 billion tons. I thought about having it mounted, but I couldn't drag it home.

I couldn't believe it. Two shots in 30 minutes, and all I had to show for it was a dead tree and a fatally wounded planet. I felt even worse when I realized I had used a 20-yard pin for a 15-yard shot. Plus, shaking like Barney Fife didn't help much either.

As promised, I headed back toward my son Nathan's stand about 9:00 AM. I didn't want to hurry through the woods. Instead, I wanted to move slowly enough to cause any deer that might move in front of me to do so in a walk and not a run. So I eased along as quietly as I could.

Not only in the art of deer hunting is the advice of others a valuable treasure, but even more it is necessary to accept guidance in areas of life beyond the woods.

I knew I was about 200 yards from Nathan when I came near a little rise. Suddenly, two deer that were bedded down stood up about 20 yards away. I was behind some brush with the wind in my face. The two deer just stood there trying to figure out what I was. They each lowered their head, then quickly popped back up to see if I would move. Somehow I managed to remain motionless on the outside. On the inside, however, I was quivering like Jell-O on a jackhammer. Amazingly, they both took a few steps and simultaneously stepped behind trees that concealed me from their eyes. I raised my bow and pulled back. As I came to full draw, the thought came to me, *Three shots in one morning? This can't be true! No pressure now because no one would believe this anyway!* The one on the left, a young buck, had moved into the clear and was looking down the hill. I let the arrow go and heard the "thud" that occurs when an arrow connects. By then my heart was pounding and I was breathing hard. I dropped my bow to my side and listened. I could hear the crashing, and I had a feeling Nathan did, too.

When I got to the truck, I couldn't believe my eyes. What I saw was unbelievable. Nathan was standing over a huge doe he had arrowed around 8:15 AM. It was his first bow hunt and his first full draw at a live deer. I had heard of these kinds of beginner stories, but only in far-off hunting grounds. But here was an actual tale waiting to be told.

> Every day in the cold, clear weather we tramped miles and miles through the woods and mountains, which, after a snow-storm took on a really wintry look; while in the moonlight the snow-laden forests shone and sparkled like crystal. The dweller in cities has but a faint idea of the way we ate and slept.
>
> *Theodore Roosevelt*

Nathan got even more excited when I told him I had a deer down, for he knew it was my first as well. We stood there on that warm September morning basking in the glow of the turn of events. To make the memory even more special, when I later tracked my animal to its final resting place, I discovered that both deer had lain down about ten yards apart.

We must have told each other the story 20 times that day. And each time we recalled something new. I'm sure we'll tell it many more times, and with each rendition the deer will get bigger, the shots longer, and my two errant arrows will sink further into the "leaves" of forgetfulness.

I'm glad I've been able to make these kinds of memories with Nathan. Our hunting experiences have provided some great father/son time. From the teaching of the safety rules of firing a weapon to the sound of the alarm clock that wakes us up on the first morning of season, we have gathered much to talk about.

THE SCOPE OF LIFE LESSONS

Up on the mountain, Nathan and I changed into dry clothes again. My heart was racing a little with anticipation as we went to the new stand I had chosen. About ten minutes before daylight we sat down . . . and the wait began. Around 8:05 AM we heard a real reason to get excited. This noise wasn't chipmunks or squirrels. This sound was different. The leaves had that certain crunch. A buck grunted. In another moment the deer we could not yet see would probably emerge on the flat just below us.

Nathan began to shake with "buck fever." I whispered, "Get ready." We waited as blood rang in my ears.

Suddenly the woods exploded with the blast of a high-powered rifle. Probably a 30-06. Crashing hooves went in all directions. In a moment, everything was silent. And then, in the distance, we heard the telltale snort.

We sat there devastated. Someone had shot "our" deer. Yet we were oddly excited that "something" had happened so close to us.

For my son, that day it was "the one that got away." The same deep disappointment comes for all.

I was grateful to have been there for him when it happened— again. I was able to let him know that the rest of life would not be much different. There would be other disappointments to face, more dreams shattered, and the inevitable feelings of resentment and betrayal that would likely accompany them. From personal experience, I knew the temptation to seek revenge and the desire to give up would crop up again somewhere along the way. However, I told him that when those hard times came, it would be important to confess those feelings to a brother like we had done that day with our tears. I told him that the only way to stop the destructive cycle of ill feelings that often lead to greater trouble was to forgive. I prayed for Nathan that night as he slept that somehow the day's disappointments would yield the fruit of longsuffering in other areas of his life. I also thanked God for the opportunity to learn important lessons like these while deer hunting with my son.

Oh, Father in heaven,

Make me to be a fine-tuned bow in Your hands.

Use my life to make the arrows You have given me to fly

accurately and confidently to the destination

You have chosen.

Help me to bend well under the tension of parenting.

And someday, should that incredible miracle happen,

and You turn my arrows into bows,

may they too understand the act of letting go.

In Jesus' name, amen.

Jos. Hautman '96

AN EASY TARGET

It was about 9 ᴀᴍ on a late November morning, and I had not spotted anything even resembling a deer. I was somewhat discouraged and was beginning the mental process of forming plans for the afternoon hunt when suddenly, from the east, I heard a crashing. Oh, how I love that sound! Talk about an adrenaline rush! Just put an IV in my vein when the crashing of deer hooves thunders through the woods, and I can produce a gallon of adrenaline.

Realizing the deer were headed my way, I quickly pulled my rifle to my shoulder and slipped the safety off. I carefully took aim at the buck. He was running right to left on a flat a mere 40 yards away from my stand. With a tremendous blast of the 30-06, I sent a "shaftless arrow" toward him, then number two "torpedo" was delivered. Both deer just kept running. I could tell by the two craters in the ground that I didn't even touch him. I wondered how I could have missed a shot that close.

As they bounded off, I stood there in that treestand totally exasperated. I was also a little perturbed at the buck. I had fired a major high-powered cannon at this guy, and he didn't even look my way. He refused to acknowledge my existence. My valiant attempt went totally unnoticed. I could've been playing a piano in that treestand, and it wouldn't have mattered to him!

But suddenly my mental reverie was interrupted. It was another sound of crashing. Lo and behold, there they came again! It was the same two deer. This time they were running from my left to right. I couldn't believe it. It occurred to me that the old buck might not have known or even cared that I was there but, hey, that doe must have known. I kind of think she was bringing him back by me. "Bless her heart! She's giving me another chance," I said

to myself. In fact, I do believe I heard a female voice as they were crashing through the second time screaming "Shoot him! Shoot him!" (Not really.) I readied, I aimed, I fired. I missed! Two more chances buried in the dirt. Four strikes and I was out. Once again, I had shot the underside of Australia.

Nursing no wounds, that buck ran off into the distance and left me to drown in the sea of disappointment. I tried to settle down, just in case they came blasting through again. I checked my rifle safety, reloaded, and checked to see if I had brought my portable plastic-bottle potty with me. I needed it by then. As I was regrouping and assuming that I wouldn't see another deer for six months, I had a sobering thought.

Though acting on instinct, that buck had cast aside its normal self-protective use of his big ears and keen sense of smell. All that was crucial for his survival in the wild was traded for a chase. A deer's "rut" or mating season lasts four or five weeks of the year, and it is not unusual for the white-tailed buck to act crazy during this period. He may have been acting normally, but in regard to his own safety and his usual overly cautious nature, he was acting like a fool. The bottom line is that, while in "rut," a buck sure makes an easy target of himself.

That's when the word *men* came to my mind. Men can act just as crazy. Just like that buck acted foolishly chasing that doe, men can make themselves just as vulnerable when they cast aside reason and wisdom and chase after something. For us men, it is so easy to set our sights on a desire and forge ahead in hot pursuit, forgetting about everything else that matters. Whether it's a boat and a largemouth bass, a gun and a grunt call, the fountain of fame, another deal that makes another dollar, or a woman at the workplace, if it causes a man to drop his guard and compromise his values, he is placing himself in a dangerous situation. When pressures or stress or temptation overwhelm a man, it becomes open season on his loyalties to other important responsibilities, and the "enemy" of all that is good will take some shots—sometimes deadly if we're not prepared.

These modern ingenious sciences and arts do not affect me as those more venerable arts of hunting and fishing, and even of husbandry in its primitive and simple form; as ancient and honorable trades as the sun and moon and winds pursue, coeval with the faculties of man, and invented when these were invented.

Henry David Thoreau

I LIKE the hunting of the hare
Better than that of the fox;
I like the joyous morning air,
And the crowing of the cocks.

I like the calm of the early fields,
The ducks asleep by the lake,
The quiet hour which Nature yields
Before mankind is awake.

I like the pheasants and feeding things
Of the unsuspicious morn;
I like the flap of the wood-pigeon's wings
As she rises from the corn.

I like the blackbird's shriek, and his rush
From the turnips as I pass by,
And the partridge hiding her head in a bush,
For her young ones cannot fly.

I like these things, and I like to ride,
When all the world is in bed,
To the top of the hill where the sky grows wide,
And where the sun grows red.

Wilfrid Scawen Blunt
"The Old Squire"

A BOUNTY OF WISDOM

The place I had chosen to hunt was on the remote west end of the property away from houses and humans. My stand was well placed. There were deer signs all around. The weather was great, and I had a 30-06 bolt action that was sighted in and could make three shot patterns the size of a half dollar at 100 yards. I was ready! However, at the end of the third day, I hadn't fired a shot. I didn't understand it. I hadn't seen one single deer.

By the time the fourth and final morning rolled around, I didn't have much hope as I trudged back to the same stand.

When 10:30 AM came and still no whitetails appeared, I packed up my gear and headed back.

I returned to my in-laws' house for lunch, and Mr. Williamson joined me at the table. He could tell I was frustrated coming back each day without filling my tag, so he offered me some advice. He said, "Steve, if you want to see deer, I suggest you hunt up here behind the house. Quite often I've seen a buck or two come out right at the corner of the fence on top of the hill. Hardly anyone has hunted around the house. I recommend you walk into the woods about 75 paces and set up facing away from the field. Around 4:30, be watching."

Within 15 minutes I heard a familiar sound—the light crunching of deer hooves pressing into the dry November leaves. Sure enough, there he came. I watched the buck for a few

minutes. Finally, his eyes disappeared behind a tree and I slowly raised my rifle. I took aim on his vitals and pulled the trigger.

The buck dropped a few yards from where he was standing when the shot was fired. I took in a deep sigh of relief, for it all seemed to happen so fast, and I needed to gather my thoughts. Then I remembered that a part of the process of harvesting an animal is to record the time of the kill on the game tag. I found my pen, and just as I was writing down the time, it hit me. My watch said 4:35. The shot was made about five minutes before, which put it right at 4:30 PM. Mr. Williamson's words echoed through my head. I sat there amazed.

As I stood there looking at the nice-size buck, I was grateful for my father-in-law's advice. Also, I was glad I had chosen to follow it. I shiver to think what I would have missed had I not been willing to listen to him. It was necessary for my success. In fact, any knowledge I possess of hunting is simply a collection of bits of wisdom I have gleaned from other hunters through the years. From conversations in pickup trucks over a thermos of hot coffee to the informative articles in the hundreds of outdoor magazines I've read, I've managed to gather enough know-how to be a successful deer hunter in nearly all of the 30-plus seasons I've ventured out into the woods to enjoy.

THE FINEST BULL, with the best head that I got, was killed in the midst of very beautiful and grand surroundings. We had been hunting through a great pine wood which ran up to the edge of a broad canyon-like valley, bounded by sheer walls of rock. There were fresh tracks of elk about, and we had been advancing up wind with even more than our usual caution when, on stepping out into a patch of open ground, near the edge of the cliff, we came upon a great bull, beating and thrashing his antlers against a young tree, about eighty yards off. He stopped and faced us for a second, his mighty antlers thrown in the air, as he held his head aloft. Behind him towered the tall and sombre pines, while at his feet the jutting crags overhung the deep chasm below, that stretched off between high walls of barren and snow-streaked rocks, the evergreens clinging to their sides, while along the bottom the rapid torrent gathered in places into black and sullen mountain lakes. As the bull turned to run I struck him just behind the shoulder; he reeled to the death-blow, but staggered gamely on a few rods into the forest before sinking to the ground, with my second bullet through his lungs.

Theodore Roosevelt
Hunting Trips of a Ranchman

James Hautman ©

"You've never climbed it?"

"I've been on the sides

Deer-hunting and trout-fishing. There's a brook

That starts up on it somewhere—I've heard say

Right on the top, tip-top—a curious thing.

But what would interest you about the brook,

It's always cold in summer, warm in winter.

One of the great sights going is to see

It steam in winter like an ox's breath,

Until the bushes all along its banks

Are inch-deep with the frosty spines and bristles—

You know the kind. Then let the sun shine on it!"

Robert Frost
"The Mountain"

© James Hautman

IN THE TWINKLING OF AN EYE...

One of the most amazing things about white-tailed deer is the uncanny ability they have to simply appear out of nowhere. With no noise, no hint of their presence, or any warning to help you brace yourself for the shock of turning your head and seeing them just standing there looking at you, they suddenly appear.

In that awesome instant, the heart rate races from 60 to 120 in zero seconds. The eyes quickly enlarge, the jaw sets, and the brain kicks into overdrive trying to figure out how to get your rigid body to respond to its commands. This is one of my favorite parts of going deer hunting.

Ode to My Hunting Friend

You taught me everything I know
About the rabbit, buck, and doe
But there's one thing you knew I'd never learn
To say, "No," to the sound
Of the wild calling me to return.

If I could walk these waters to the shore
But this ship has gone too far and then some more
Someday I'll be back in the woods again,
But until then pray for me, your huntin' friend.
                                    Steve Chapman

WHILE I LOVE TO HEAR the sweetness of Annie's voice, the children saying "Dad," a congregation singing "It Is Well With My Soul," the lilting brilliance of a hammered dulcimer, the "Andy Griffith Show" theme song, and many other sounds, I would add to that list the distinctive, telltale, slight crunch of the leaves that a deer hoof makes. Somehow, I've developed a keen ability to distinguish it from the scamper of a squirrel or any other noise in the woods.

A Hunter's Promise

I, beside this quiet doe
Kneel and for a minute mourn
Between my victory and her woe
My quickly beating heart is torn.

I, on this mountain midst the oaks
Vow to this beast that once had life
We will give thanks when down below
We taste your strength...
Your sacrifice.

Steve Chapman